The Cat

Illustrations : Pascale Wirth
Text : Nadine Saunier

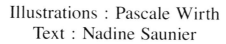

BARRON'S

New York • London • Toronto • Sydney

The cat is a beautiful   come to life.
She is curious and explores everywhere.
But she is also cautious
and never passes through an
opening smaller than her long   .

She can see quite well in the dark,
but she can't distinguish all of the colors.

A cat's fur is

either spotted or   .
The fur protects her from insect bites,
thorns, and the cold.
The alley cat is often bigger and meaner
than its pedigree cousins:
the Angora and the Siamese.
The Siamese is often
called the "prince of cats."
The Sphynx is a very unusual cat: he doesn't
have one bit of   on his entire body.

Cats are not afraid of heights.
They jump on rooftops
and from eaves to gutters,

just like  !

If they fall, they land safely, thanks to the little
cushions on the bottoms of their paws.

Puff is a lazybones.
She sleeps or dozes twelve hours a day.
In the house, she has her own corner, with

an old

and some thick

She claws them and rubs against
them, purring all the while.

Puss loves to eat.

He chases  ,

rats, and birds.
He plays with them
but doesn't always eat them.

He's a patient  ,

who loves the taste of fresh .
The smell of green plants,
makes him wild with joy.
He feasts on catnip,
which cleans his stomach.

After a meal, Puff licks herself clean.
Her tongue is as rough

as a .

She
smooths the fur of her ,
wets her paw with saliva,
then passes it over her head,
on her cheeks, and behind her ears.
She works hard to make herself beautiful!

At night, cats roam.
The males and females meet.
Their meowing, their mating cries, and
their purring seem to have no end.
Two months later,

the  are born.

Kittens are born
with their eyes closed.
At first they nurse from their mother's nipples.
But when they are just six weeks old,
they can feed themselves.

They are good little
who love to frolic.
Cats usually live to be fifteen years old.

Kittens are almost too cute.
They lie in wait, then pounce and bite.

They love to play with a ,

a , a ,

a or anything else that moves.

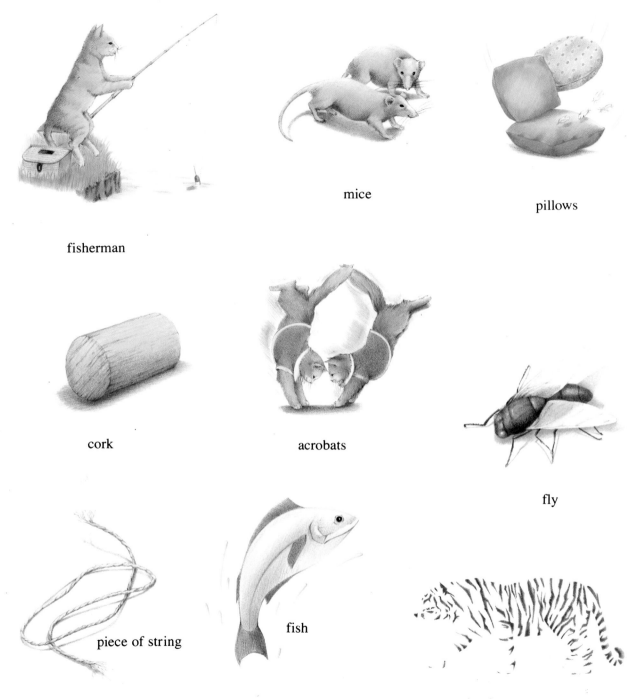

fisherman

mice

pillows

cork

acrobats

fly

piece of string

fish

striped